Black
AND
British

DAVID OLUSOGA

Black AND British

An illustrated history

Illustrated by
Jake Alexander & Melleny Taylor

MACMILLAN CHILDREN'S BOOKS

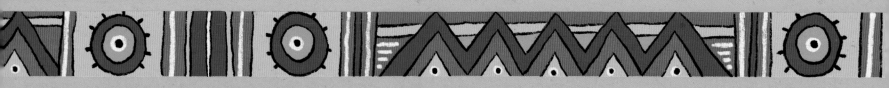

For my beloved daughter.

Published 2021 by Macmillan Children's Books
an imprint of Pan Macmillan
The Smithson, 6 Briset Street, London EC1M 5NR
EU representative: Macmillan Publishers Ireland Ltd, 1st Floor,
The Liffey Trust Centre, 117–126 Sheriff Street Upper
Dublin 1, D01 YC43
Associated companies throughout the world
www.panmacmillan.com

ISBN 978-1-5290-5295-4

1 3 5 7 9 8 6 4 2

A CIP catalogue record for this book is available from the British Library.

Printed and bound in Italy by L.E.G.O. S.p.A.

Design: Becky Chilcott
Editorial: Jo Foster

Contents

✴ INTRODUCTION 6

✴ THE ROMANS 8

✴ THE TUDORS 12

✴ THE STUARTS 20

✴ THE GEORGIANS 26

✴ THE VICTORIANS 42

✴ THE FIRST WORLD WAR...58

✴ THE SECOND WORLD WAR 62

✴ WINDRUSH TO TODAY...66

✴ AFTERWORD...74

✴ GLOSSARY 76

✴ ABOUT THE AUTHOR & ILLUSTRATORS 80

INTRODUCTION

A few years ago I wrote a book for grown-ups about Black British history. Since I finished writing that book, young people and their parents have been asking me to write a version for children. That is why I have written this book. It is the book I wish I had been given at school.

When I was at school there was no Black history. None of the Black people from the past who we know about today were ever mentioned by my teachers, and my textbooks contained nothing about the role Black people have played in the story of Britain. So what I presumed was that there must not have been any Black people in British history.

It was only when I became a teenager, and was able to read grown-up history books, that I learned that there had been Black people throughout much of British history, all the way back to the Roman conquest. It was from then onwards that I learned about slavery and about the British Empire, about Black Tudors, like the trumpeter John Blanke, and Black people like Dido Elizabeth Belle and Olaudah Equiano who lived in Britain in the eighteenth century. I also learned about the Black children who lived as slaves in the houses of rich people in London, Bristol, Liverpool and other cities. I read about the enslaved people who were made to work on plantations in the West Indies and America, and learned how the

sugar and cotton they grew helped make Britain rich. I discovered that there had been Black sailors at the Battle of Trafalgar and that Black soldiers had fought in the trenches of the First World War. I read about the Black pilots and navigators who served in the Royal Air Force during the Second World War and about the people who had come to Britain on the *Windrush* in 1948 to start new lives.

I wish I had been taught all of this as a child. And there are so many more stories to explore, so many other Black people who made their homes in Britain in past centuries whom historians have not yet discovered.

With each passing year, Black British history is becoming ever more personal to increasing numbers of people. Britain's population is changing. More of us than ever are members of families that include people of different skin colours and ethnicities. Black history helps explain how national history is intertwined with our family histories. It helps us make sense of the country we are today.

DAVID OLUSOGA

THE ROMANS

An empire is a large group of states or countries controlled by one powerful ruler or government.

Africans first came to Britain with the Roman Empire. Long before Britain began to build its own empire, it was invaded and conquered by the Romans. Britain became a part of the mighty empire of Rome, which stretched across Europe, North Africa, and the Middle East.

The Roman Empire 117 AD

Hadrian's Wall

Britannia

Belgica

Germania Superior

Noricum

Aquitania   Raetia   Pannonia   Dacia

Narbonensis   Dalmatia   Moesia

Italia

Tarraconensis   •Rome   Thracia

Macedonia   Armenia

Lusitania   Galatia   Cappadocia

Asia

Baetica   Lycia   Assyria

Cilicia

Mauretania   Africa   Syria   Mesopotamia

Cyprus

Judaea

Cyrenaica

Aegyptus

When we talk about the Romans who came to Britain, we don't just mean people from Rome or Italy. Roman citizens could come from anywhere in the empire, and they moved around it like never before. People from all over the empire travelled huge distances to trade, work, and fight in the Roman army. This included people from Africa who came to Roman Britain.

55 and 54 BC

Julius Caesar tries twice to invade Britain, but fails each time.

43 AD

Emperor Claudius successfully invades and begins Roman rule in Britain.

60 AD

Boudicca leads a rebellion against the Romans.

71 AD

The city of Eboracum (today's York) is founded.

About 409 AD

Roman rule over Britain ends. The pathways between Britain and Africa are wiped away. For the next thousand years, only a few Africans come to Britain.

122 AD

The Emperor Hadrian visits Britain and orders a wall to be built across northern England.

138 AD

Quintus Lollius Urbicus, from North Africa, is governor of the Roman province of Britannia.

211 AD

Emperor Septimus Severus, who was born in Africa, dies in York.

253–258 AD

An African unit of Roman soldiers is stationed on Hadrian's Wall.

306 AD

Constantine I is proclaimed Emperor at York.

Hadrian's Wall

Cataractonium (Catterick)

Mamucium (Manchester)

Eboracum (York)

Lindum (Lincoln)

Venonis (High Cross, Leicestershire)

Venta Icenorum (Caistor)

Isca (Caerleon)

Glevum (Gloucester)

Camulodunum (Colchester)

Venta Belgarum (Winchester)

Isca Dumnoniorum (Exeter)

Durnovaria (Dorchester)

Londinium (London)

Aurelian Moors

The first recorded group of Africans living in Britain were soldiers in the Roman army. They came to defend the edge of the empire at Hadrian's Wall. The wall stretched for more than seventy miles, right across what is now northern England. Soldiers were stationed along the wall.

One unit of soldiers called the 'Aurelian Moors' was stationed at the fortress of Aballava on Hadrian's Wall in the third century. The word 'moors' shows where they came from: it means 'people from North Africa'. Aballava wasn't just a fort; it was a whole community. As well as soldiers and officers, other people from across the empire would have lived in Aballava, including the soldiers' families.

Roman York

In Roman times, York was known as Eboracum. It was one of the most important cities in Roman Britain, and had a very diverse population. Archaeologists have found that many people in Roman York had African ancestors.

'Ivory Bangle Lady', who is believed to be mixed-race, is one Roman whose skeleton was found in York.

Ivory Bangle Lady was a rich young woman. She was buried with expensive luxuries including black and white bangles. The black bangles were made of local jet, and the white bangles were made of ivory, possibly from Africa.

From studying Ivory Bangle Lady's skull and the chemicals in her bones, archaeologists found she was probably mixed-race, with a North African background, and she didn't grow up in York.

It wouldn't have seemed odd to a Roman that Ivory Bangle Lady was both African and rich. The skeletons of African Romans have been found in York in places where both rich and poor people were buried. Romans didn't think and write about race and skin colour in the same way we do today.

THE TUDORS

King Henry VII

King Henry VIII

After Roman rule in Britain ended, connections with Africa were weakened for hundreds of years. The next time we see records of many Black people living in Britain was when the Tudors ruled England.

The first King of England from the Tudor dynasty was Henry VII, who was crowned in 1485. His son ruled as King Henry VIII.

In Tudor times, Britain's links with the outside world were growing. Europeans were making more journeys to Africa, and so more Africans began to come to Britain: some from Europe, some from the Americas, and some direct from Africa.

Trumpeter John Blanke plays at the Westminster Tournament, a royal celebration for Henry VIII.

John Blanke

John Blanke is the earliest Black person in Britain whose name and face we know. He was a trumpeter in the Tudor Royal Court.

John was right at the centre of historic Tudor events. He played at King Henry VII's funeral, and at his son King Henry VIII's coronation. John also played at a two-day celebration in 1511 called the Westminster Tournament. The King held the tournament to celebrate the birth of his son (sadly, the baby prince would only live for a few weeks). In the pictures painted to record the celebration, you can see the face of John Blanke among the trumpet players.

As a musician, John Blanke had a skilled job and he knew his own worth. He wrote to Henry VIII to ask for a pay rise, so that he would be on the same level as the other trumpeters. When John got married, the King sent him a new outfit as a wedding present.

We don't know where John Blanke grew up but many of the Black people in Britain came from countries in southern Europe with more contact and trade with Africa, like Spain, Portugal, or Italy.

Henry VIII's first wife, Catherine of Aragon, was Spanish. When she came to England in 1501 she brought a whole group of servants and followers with her, including Africans. European royals liked to show off their modern international connections by employing African musicians and servants.

The Tudors ruled over England and Wales, not the whole of Great Britain. England and Scotland were not ruled by the same King until 1603.

Jacques Francis

Jacques Francis was a diver who helped to bring up valuables from the sunken wreck of King Henry VIII's ship, the *Mary Rose*. Jacques came to England as part of an expert diving team run by an Italian.

Jacques was born on an island off the coast of West Africa. People in that area were skilled swimmers, and some learned to dive deep underwater to collect shells and pearls or to find sunken treasure from shipwrecks. Most English people at this time could not swim, so African divers were seen as very brave.

The *Mary Rose* sank near Portsmouth in 1545. Soon afterwards, King Henry hired divers to get back the expensive weapons that had sunk with the ship. Jacques and his teammates dived to the bottom of the murky water to bring up as many of the ship's guns as they could.

We know about the story of Jacques Francis from court records that have survived. When he acted as a witness, the other side argued that the word of a slave from a non-Christian country didn't count. But Jacques was not enslaved: he was paid for his work. Slavery was legal in Italy, where Jacques' boss came from, but not in England.

Historians have found records of hundreds of Black people living in Tudor England. They worked in a range of jobs, and many married and had children.

Mary Fillis

Mary Fillis was born in Morocco. She came to London at the age of 6 or 7, and worked as a servant for a merchant's family before finding work with a seamstress (a woman who sewed clothes).

In 1597, Mary was baptized in her local church. She was a young woman by this time. On the baptism record, Mary was described as a 'black more', a Tudor term for Black person.

Mary would have seen other Black people living around her in London. Records show that other Africans were also baptized and buried in her area, and even worked for the same family as Mary.

Baptism

Baptism is a ceremony in which someone becomes a member of the Christian Church. Religion was very important in Tudor times. For someone like Mary Fillis, baptism showed everyone that she was truly a part of her community.

Africans like Jacques Francis and Mary Fillis would have stood out as unusual because of their appearance. But religion, and how rich or poor a person was, may have been more important than their skin colour in Tudor times.

More than fifty years before the Tudors took power in England, European sailors began to explore the world and to brave the dangerous seas around West Africa.

Ocean-going ships in Lisbon harbour, Portugal

Portuguese traders were the first Europeans to venture south of the Mediterranean to the West African coast by sea. Portuguese sailors had the most advanced ships, and they used science learned from the Muslim world to find their way. This meant they could beat their European rivals and control the trade which would bring them riches.

William Hawkins

When the English heard about the wealth brought from Africa by Portuguese traders, they wanted some of it for themselves. In the 1530s an English sea captain named William Hawkins sailed to West Africa and then on to Brazil.

Thomas Wyndham

In 1553 Thomas Wyndham, an English captain and former pirate, joined forces with an experienced Portuguese sailor called Anthony Anes Pinteado for his voyage to West Africa.

Wyndham attacked and robbed Portuguese ships and bases, and also managed to trade with the Africans for gold and pepper. When Pinteado said they should head home, Wyndham didn't listen. They, along with two thirds of their crew, died of fever before they made it back to London. Despite this, the profits proved that trading with Africa could be worth the risk. More English traders began to sail to West Africa.

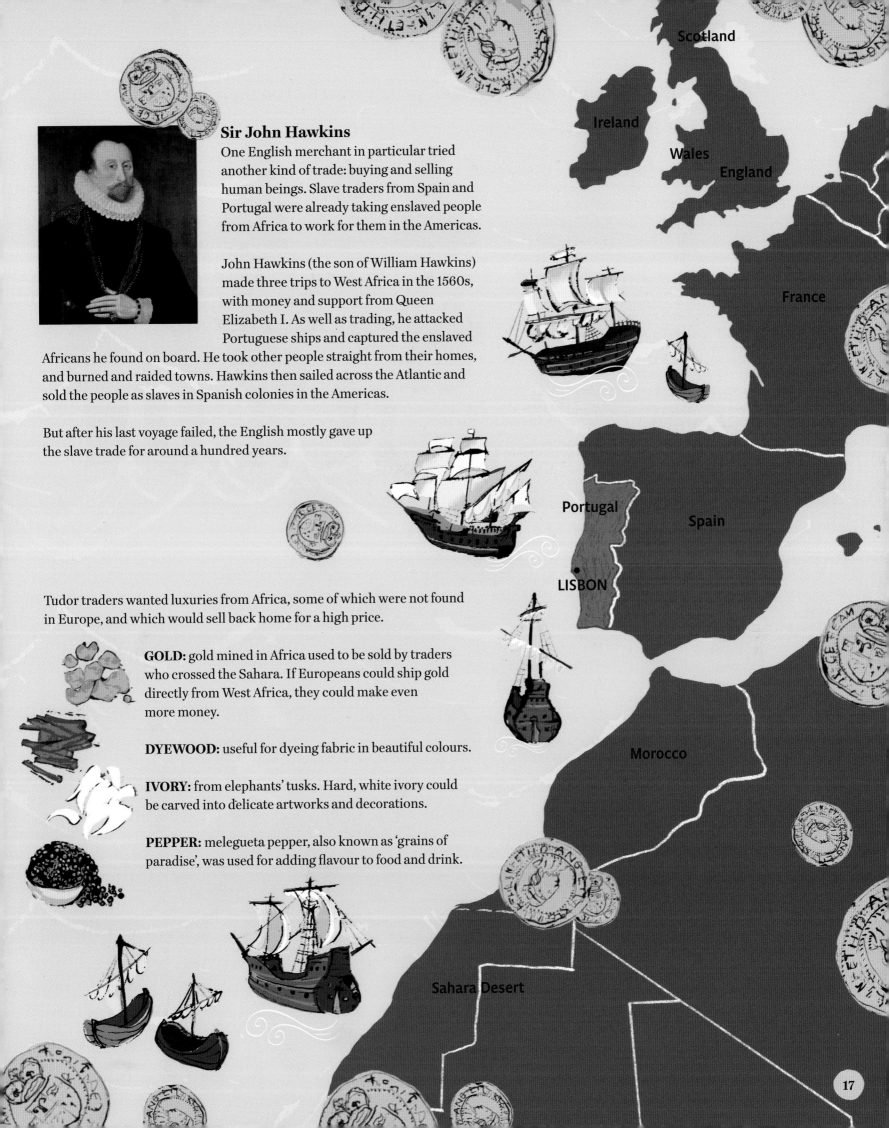

Sir John Hawkins

One English merchant in particular tried another kind of trade: buying and selling human beings. Slave traders from Spain and Portugal were already taking enslaved people from Africa to work for them in the Americas.

John Hawkins (the son of William Hawkins) made three trips to West Africa in the 1560s, with money and support from Queen Elizabeth I. As well as trading, he attacked Portuguese ships and captured the enslaved Africans he found on board. He took other people straight from their homes, and burned and raided towns. Hawkins then sailed across the Atlantic and sold the people as slaves in Spanish colonies in the Americas.

But after his last voyage failed, the English mostly gave up the slave trade for around a hundred years.

Tudor traders wanted luxuries from Africa, some of which were not found in Europe, and which would sell back home for a high price.

GOLD: gold mined in Africa used to be sold by traders who crossed the Sahara. If Europeans could ship gold directly from West Africa, they could make even more money.

DYEWOOD: useful for dyeing fabric in beautiful colours.

IVORY: from elephants' tusks. Hard, white ivory could be carved into delicate artworks and decorations.

PEPPER: melegueta pepper, also known as 'grains of paradise', was used for adding flavour to food and drink.

Scotland

Ireland

Wales

England

France

Portugal

Spain

LISBON

Morocco

Sahara Desert

17

Once ships were going from England to Africa, people travelled on them in both directions.

Five men from the village of Shama in modern-day Ghana came to London in the 1550s with the English captain John Lok. We know the English names that three of them used: Anthonie, Binnie and George. They were described later as 'tall and strong men', who coped well enough with English food and drink, but did not appreciate the cold, damp weather.

The five men spent a few months in London and learned English before going home. The plan was that they would be able to work as interpreters and help English traders make deals with the locals.

If the English wanted African gold, they needed to work with experienced traders. The West African kingdoms were rich, and had been trading with outsiders for centuries. They knew exactly how valuable their gold was, and they had strong leaders and powerful armies.

SIXTEENTH CENTURY WEST AFRICAN KINGDOMS

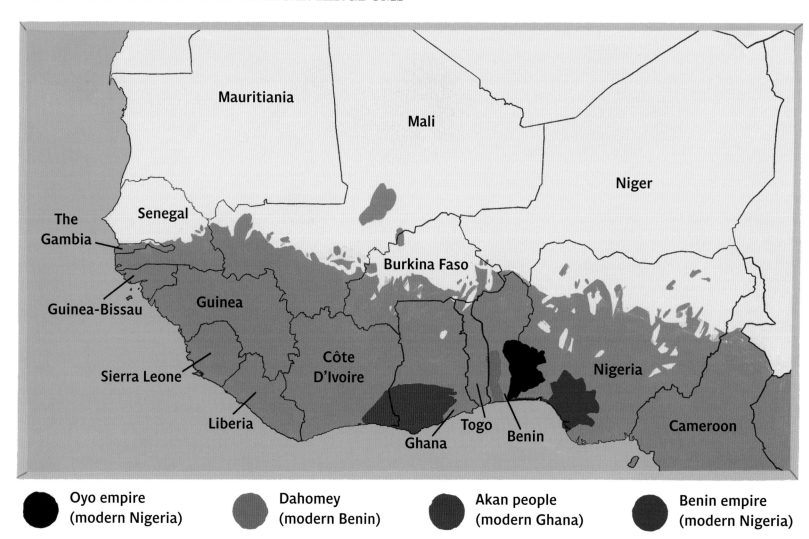

Mauritiania

Mali

Niger

Senegal

The Gambia

Burkina Faso

Guinea-Bissau

Guinea

Sierra Leone

Côte D'Ivoire

Nigeria

Liberia

Togo

Benin

Cameroon

Ghana

- ● Oyo empire (modern Nigeria)
- ● Dahomey (modern Benin)
- ● Akan people (modern Ghana)
- ● Benin empire (modern Nigeria)

Diego was an African man enslaved by the Spanish in Panama when English ships arrived in 1572 to raid his town, led by Francis Drake.

Diego arranged for Drake to meet the leader of the Cimaroons, a group of Africans who had escaped from the Spanish.

The Cimaroons agreed to work with Drake against their shared enemy, and together they raided the Spanish for silver. When Drake's crew went back to England, Diego went with them.

Francis Drake was one of the most famous sea captains of Tudor times. He was knighted by Queen Elizabeth I, and helped to defeat the Spanish Armada's attack on England in 1588.

He was also the first English man to captain a voyage around the world.

Francis Drake set out on this voyage in 1577. On board was Diego, working as Drake's trusted personal servant. He spoke both Spanish and English, and had been extremely helpful to Drake before. Sadly, after two years of adventures, Diego died before the voyage ended.

Other Africans sailed with Drake on his voyage around the world too. They were not all treated as well as Diego. Although he respected Diego and the Cimaroons, Drake had bought and sold enslaved Africans on past voyages.

The Drake Jewel

Queen Elizabeth I gave Sir Francis Drake a present which shows how important Africa was to the Tudors. The 'Drake Jewel' has two carved heads on it: an African man's head in black, on top of a European's head in white.

Perhaps the African face represents Drake's friends the Cimaroons. Elizabeth wanted England to defeat the Spanish and be a great power in the world, and working together with Africans could help achieve those aims.

Sir Francis Drake

THE STUARTS

1607
English settlers began their first permanent colony in North America: Virginia. They found they could make money from farming tobacco, which grew well there.

1619
The first enslaved Africans arrived in Virginia. A famous English settler called John Rolf, who married the young woman we know as Pocahontas, recorded their arrival and described them as '20 and odd Negroes'.

1627
English settlers, or 'planters', took over the island of Barbados, one of the first British colonies in the West Indies. The valuable product they farmed on Barbados was sugar.

Sugar
Sugar cane was suited to the tropical climate of the West Indies. Back in England, people loved sugar's sweetness.

Growing and processing sugar took a lot of hard, dangerous work. After growing and harvesting the plants, workers had to squeeze juice from the cane between heavy rollers before it went sour, then get it quickly to the 'boiling house' to boil it down into raw sugar.

The planters wanted more workers than they could get from Europe, so as the farms grew they used more enslaved people from Africa. Soon the whole island of Barbados produced sugar on big farms called plantations, powered by the work of thousands of enslaved people.

In the Stuart period, Britain made new colonies on the other side of the Atlantic Ocean. Together with the Stuart royals, English merchants developed brutal new ways of making money. They built up slave-powered colonies in America and the West Indies, and grew a trade in human beings that would make Britain one of the world's biggest slave-trading countries.

Planters' laws

By 1660 there were more enslaved Africans than Europeans living on Barbados. To keep the Africans from rebelling, the planters made new laws.

1661

The Barbados Slave Code set out the rules of the new slave system. There were different rules for white and Black people, with worse punishments for enslaved Black people. An enslaved person stayed enslaved for their whole life, and their children were born enslaved too. The Code was copied by other European colonies in the Americas.

In this way, the system split people by law into two groups: enslaved Black people, and free white people. It was around this time that some English people started to think of themselves as part of a group called 'white'.

Florida

The Bahamas

Cuba

Cayman Islands

Haiti

Jamaica

Honduras

Nicaragua

The Caribbean Sea is named after the Carib people who lived in the region when Europeans first came there. After Christopher Columbus arrived in the Bahamas in 1492, European countries began to colonize the islands of the Caribbean. Spain arrived first, followed by other countries including England. These colonizing European powers called these islands the West Indies.

Costa Rica

Colombia

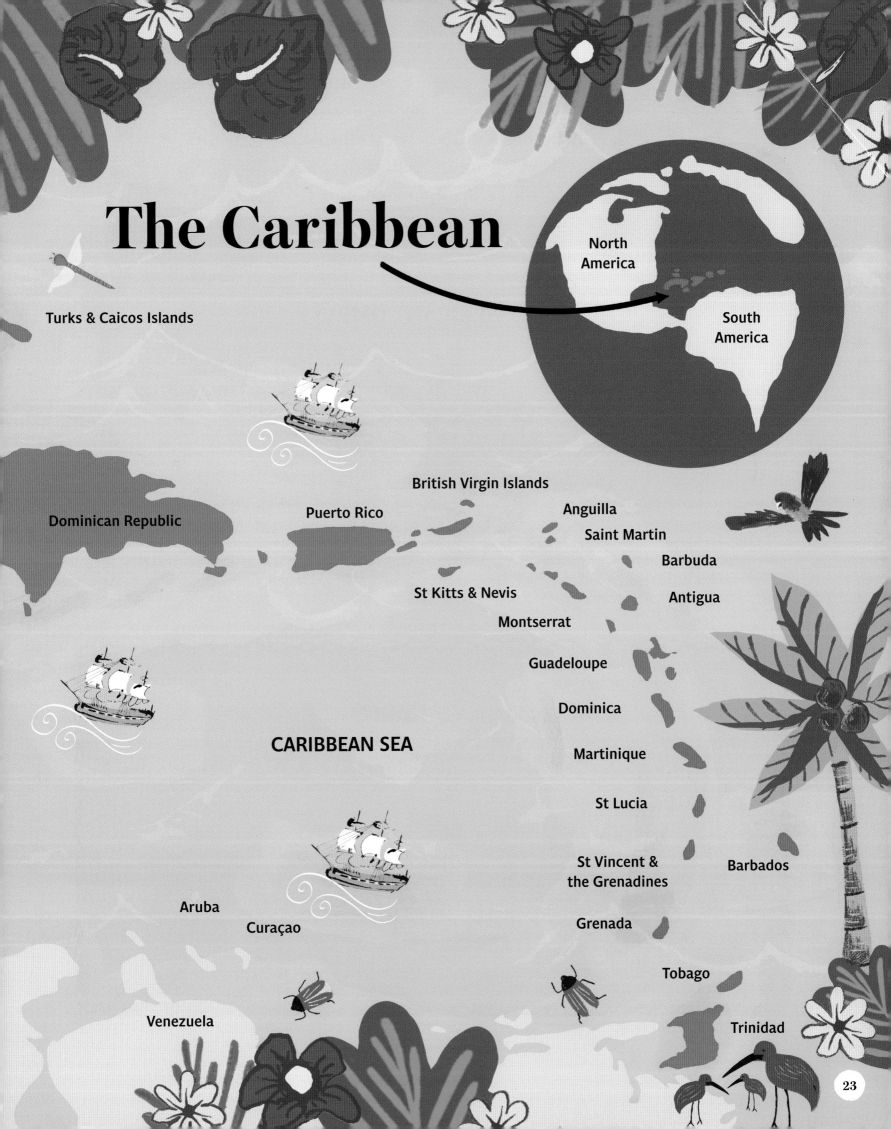

The Caribbean

North America

South America

Turks & Caicos Islands

Dominican Republic

British Virgin Islands

Puerto Rico

Anguilla

Saint Martin

Barbuda

St Kitts & Nevis

Antigua

Montserrat

Guadeloupe

Dominica

CARIBBEAN SEA

Martinique

St Lucia

St Vincent &
the Grenadines

Barbados

Aruba

Curaçao

Grenada

Tobago

Venezuela

Trinidad

23

King Charles II

James, Duke of York

Making enslaved people work on plantations was a separate business from buying and selling people as slaves. Britain made money from both.

ROYAL AFRICAN COMPANY

At first, only a few English ships brought people from Africa to sell. Instead, English planters mostly used enslaved people bought or stolen from foreign traders.

1660
Charles II became King of England. Charles and his brother James, Duke of York, the future King James II, saw an opportunity to make money by using English ships to trade in enslaved people.

Charles and James set up a royal company which would be the only one allowed to buy and sell slaves. James, Duke of York, ran the Royal African Company as its governor.

This powerful, royal-led business brought more Africans across the Atlantic into slavery than any other British company in history.

Like other European slave traders, the Royal African Company built forts called 'slave castles' around the coast of West Africa. The people they bought from local slave traders were kept prisoner there.

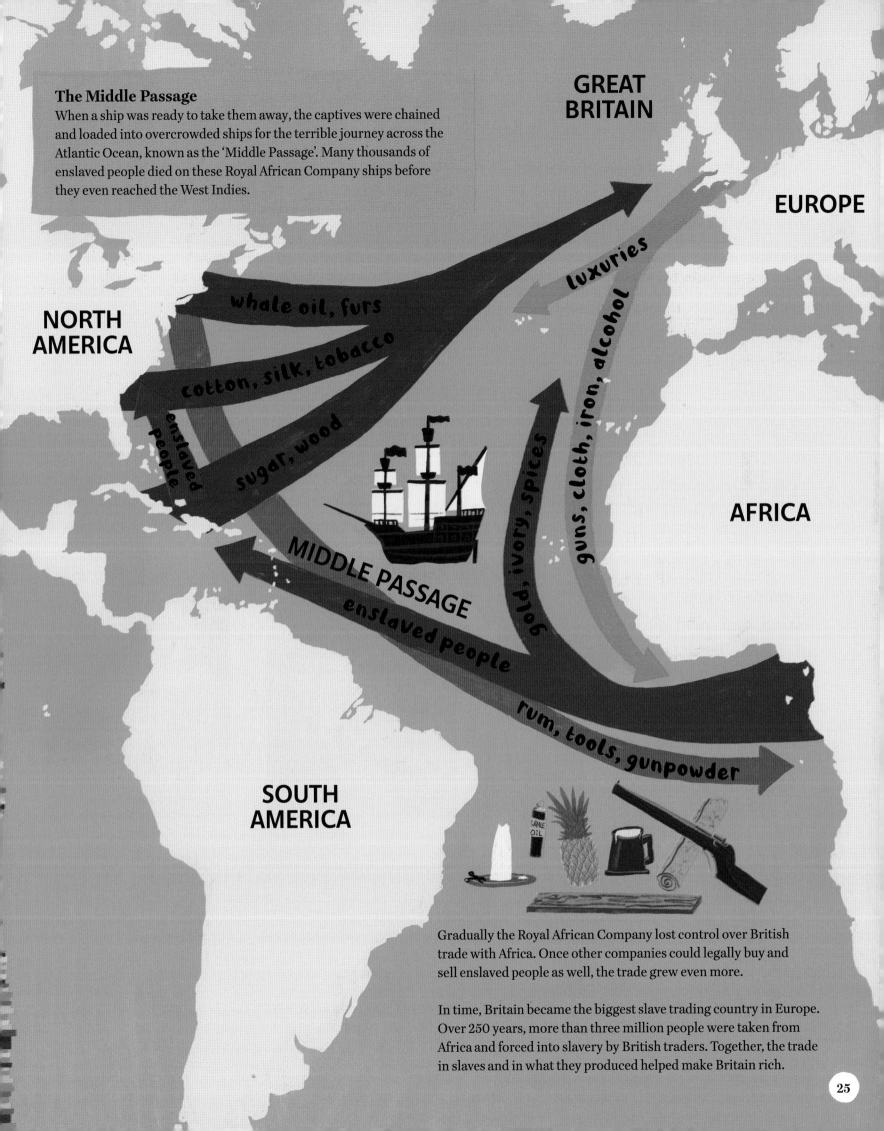

The Middle Passage
When a ship was ready to take them away, the captives were chained and loaded into overcrowded ships for the terrible journey across the Atlantic Ocean, known as the 'Middle Passage'. Many thousands of enslaved people died on these Royal African Company ships before they even reached the West Indies.

GREAT BRITAIN

EUROPE

NORTH AMERICA

AFRICA

SOUTH AMERICA

whale oil, furs

cotton, silk, tobacco

sugar, wood

enslaved people

luxuries

guns, cloth, iron, alcohol

gold, ivory, spices

MIDDLE PASSAGE

enslaved people

rum, tools, gunpowder

WHALE OIL

Gradually the Royal African Company lost control over British trade with Africa. Once other companies could legally buy and sell enslaved people as well, the trade grew even more.

In time, Britain became the biggest slave trading country in Europe. Over 250 years, more than three million people were taken from Africa and forced into slavery by British traders. Together, the trade in slaves and in what they produced helped make Britain rich.

THE GEORGIANS

By the eighteenth century, Britain's colonies in North America and the Caribbean were making huge fortunes for the rich families who owned plantations there. The work on the plantations was done by enslaved Black people brought from Africa in slave ships.

Captains of slave ships could bring one or two enslaved people back from a voyage with them. Once they got to Britain, these people were often sold to rich families as servants. Many of them were very young, and most of them were boys.

Rich people who owned enslaved Black servants liked to include them in their own portraits, to show them off. You can find their faces in hundreds of paintings from the Georgian period.

The Black people in these paintings were dressed in expensive uniforms. They are sometimes shown with fashionable luxuries from Africa or Asia, like tropical fruit, pet monkeys or parrots.

You can see that the Black servants were not the important people in these paintings by the way they were painted to one side or right at the edge of the painting, usually looking at their rich owners.

The Daily Advertiser

ADVERTS like these appeared in local newspapers when there was an enslaved person for sale.

TO BE SOLD,
A healthy NEGRO SLAVE
Named PRINCE,
Seventeen Years of Age, five Feet ten Inches high, and extremely well grown, Enquire on JOSHUA SPRINGER, in St. Stephens-Lane

To be S O L D,

A Negro Servant about Sixteen Years of Age, born on the Gold Coast, from which Place he was brought five Years since. He is about five Foot four Inches high, well made, and very slight; speaks English well, and understands the Business of a Family Footman. Any Person wanting such a Servant, may be further informed by applying to the Universal Register Office, opposite Cecil-Street in the Strand.

ELOPED from Mr. Samuel DELPRATT, Merchant, at Bristol, and come to London, A NEGRO MAN, about 17 or 18 Years old, Five Feet Five or Six Inches high, had on when he left Bristol, a brown Livery Coat lined with Red, red Button Holes and Collar, red Waistcoat, a Pair of old Leather Breeches pieced at the Knee, a black Leather Cap, and a Pair of black ribbed Stockings, answers to the Name of JOHN; if he should offer to ship himself as a free Man, on Board any Ship, by directing a Line to the Jamaica Coffee House, for Capt. William Tomlinson, or to Mr. Joseph Malpas, Jeweller, in Wood Street, Cheapside, whatever Expence in stopping the said Negro shall be repaid with Thanks and Six Guineas Reward.

SOME enslaved servants in Georgian Britain tried to escape. Their owners saw this as losing valuable property. They would pay to advertise in the newspapers offering rewards to anyone who caught the runaway.

These adverts often describe the uniforms each enslaved person was made to wear. Some had to wear metal collars around their necks.

Adverts also tell us the names the runaways used. They had often been given grand Roman-sounding names such as Caesar, Scipio and Pompey.

It wasn't just runaways who had to worry about being caught. Even free Black people in Britain were in danger of being kidnapped and sent to work as slaves in the Caribbean.

E L O P E D,

The 5th of FEBRUARY, 1763,

from JOHN STONE ESQ. of CHIPPENHAM,

A NEGRO SERVANT,

Named GLOUCESTER;

Twenty-one Years of Age, about five Feet six Inches high, slender grown, marked with a long Scar down the Middle of his Forehead, and speaks English tolerably well. Whoever secures said Negro, and gives notice of it to JOHN STONE, ESQ. aforesaid, so that he may be brought back again, will be sufficiently rewarded for their Trouble.—But any Person countenancing or harbouring the said Black, will be prosecuted agreeable to the Law.

Meet some of the Black Georgians whose stories we know: from sailors to writers, and from a champion boxer to a slave-owning gentleman.

A STRIKING VIEW of RICHMOND.

1. Ignatius Sancho was a London shopkeeper, writer, and composer, who had his portrait painted by a famous artist. Ignatius was the first Black person to vote in a British general election.

2. Several Black sailors served in the Royal Navy at the historic Battle of Trafalgar. One of them is pictured on Nelson's Column.

3. Dido Elizabeth Belle was the daughter of an enslaved Black woman and a white British naval officer. She was brought up in England by her great-uncle, the judge Lord Mansfield, alongside a young white girl. Dido was loved, but not treated equally.

4. James Albert Ukawsaw Gronniosaw, born in Nigeria, was enslaved in the West Indies and North America before moving to England and marrying an English woman. James and his family moved around the country looking for work and sometimes went hungry. The book of his life story shows how many poor Black Georgians lived.

5. Bill Richmond was a famous boxer. Born near New York, he became Britain's first Black sporting celebrity.

6. Julius Soubise was enslaved to a duchess who paid for his education. He became an expert sword fighter and horse rider.

7. Phillis Wheatley was enslaved in America, but learned to read and write and became a famous poet. She visited London in 1773, where her poetry was a huge success.

8. Mary Prince was the first Black woman to publish her life story, which told how she and her sisters were sold and made to leave their mother when they were young.

9. Ottobah Cugoano was born in Ghana, enslaved in the West Indies, and then freed in London. He became a leading voice among Black Londoners, and wrote a book arguing against slavery.

10. Nathaniel Wells was the son of a white plantation owner and a Black enslaved woman. He inherited a huge fortune when his father died – meaning he legally owned enslaved people. Nathaniel lived as a country gentleman in Wales.

The American Revolution

The American Revolution was the beginning of the United States of America's independence from Britain. In 1775, American colonists known as the Patriots rebelled against British rule, and the American Revolutionary War began. By this time, around one person in every five living in British North America was an enslaved African. The British promised freedom to any enslaved men who escaped from Patriot owners and joined the British. Thousands of Black men took this chance.

Harry Washington was born in West Africa, captured and enslaved, and bought by George Washington. He ran away to join the British 'Black Pioneers' regiment in the Revolutionary War. As the war ended, Harry left New York on a British ship and went to Nova Scotia. Later, he made a new life for himself again, with a group of Black settlers in Sierra Leone – back in West Africa.

George Washington owned a plantation worked by enslaved people. He led the Patriot armies against the British, and became the first President of the USA. In 1783, George led his army into New York to end the war. He made a a list of the Black people who had escaped from him. He wanted to take them back to his plantation. Harry Washington's name was on the list, but by the time George got to New York, Harry had escaped from him again.

Shadrack Furman was a free Black man working for the British when he was captured and tortured by Patriots. After the war he survived on the streets of London by playing the violin and begging. He applied to the government fund for people who had fought for the British, and was given £18 a year – less than most white loyalists got.

Peter Anderson was a free man who was forced to fight in the British 'Ethiopian Regiment' in the war. Peter was captured by the Patriots, but escaped and joined the British again. Peter ended up poor and homeless in London, unable to go home to his family. The government finally gave him £10 after the commander of his regiment said he was telling the truth.

When the British lost the war, the 'Black loyalists' who had fought for the King had to escape or be enslaved again. They fled the United States on British ships, many to Nova Scotia in British-owned Canada. Others escaped to London, where most had no money and nowhere to live.

Freedom in Britain

Was slavery legal in Britain? This question caused fierce arguments in Georgian law courts. Some people argued that enslaved people became legally free once they arrived in Britain.

Jonathan Strong was an enslaved boy who lived in London. One day in 1765, Jonathan's owner beat him and threw him out into the street. He found his way to a doctor and his brother, William and Granville Sharp, who cared for him and found him a job.

Two years later, the man who had owned Jonathan kidnapped him and sold him to be sent to Jamaica as a slave. But Jonathan wrote to Granville Sharp asking for help and Granville helped to free him.

After meeting Jonathan Strong, Granville made it his mission in life to fight against slavery. He studied the law and wrote a book on the law and slavery. Granville looked out for a case that would force the judges to make up their minds.

The wait was over when Granville learned about James Somerset, who had escaped his owner in London and been caught.

Granville Sharp helped Somerset take his case to court, and made sure the trial got plenty of attention. The judge, Lord Mansfield, decided that James Somerset could not be kidnapped and sent to the colonies, and instead was a free man. He did not say that other slaves should also be free in England – but plenty of people thought that was what he meant.

One of the people who heard about Lord Mansfield's decision was Joseph Knight, an enslaved man in Scotland. Joseph left his owner, who later had him arrested. The Scottish courts agreed with Joseph that he was legally free.

Granville Sharp

Granville Sharp the Abolitionist Rescuing a Slave from the Hands of His Master (1864). This painting was inspired by the story of Jonathan Strong.

Abolition

Eighteenth-century Britain was addicted to sugar and to the wealth that came from using enslaved people to work on plantations. But campaigners called abolitionists began to spread the word about the truth of the slave trade and slavery, and fought to change the law.

1772
Judge Lord Mansfield decided that a Black man, James Somerset, could not be taken from England back to slavery in the colonies. Many people took this to mean that slavery was not legal in England.

1781
133 captives on the slave ship *Zong* were killed. The owners tried to claim insurance money for the loss of their property. Campaigners drew attention to the *Zong* case to reveal the terrible secrets of the slave trade.

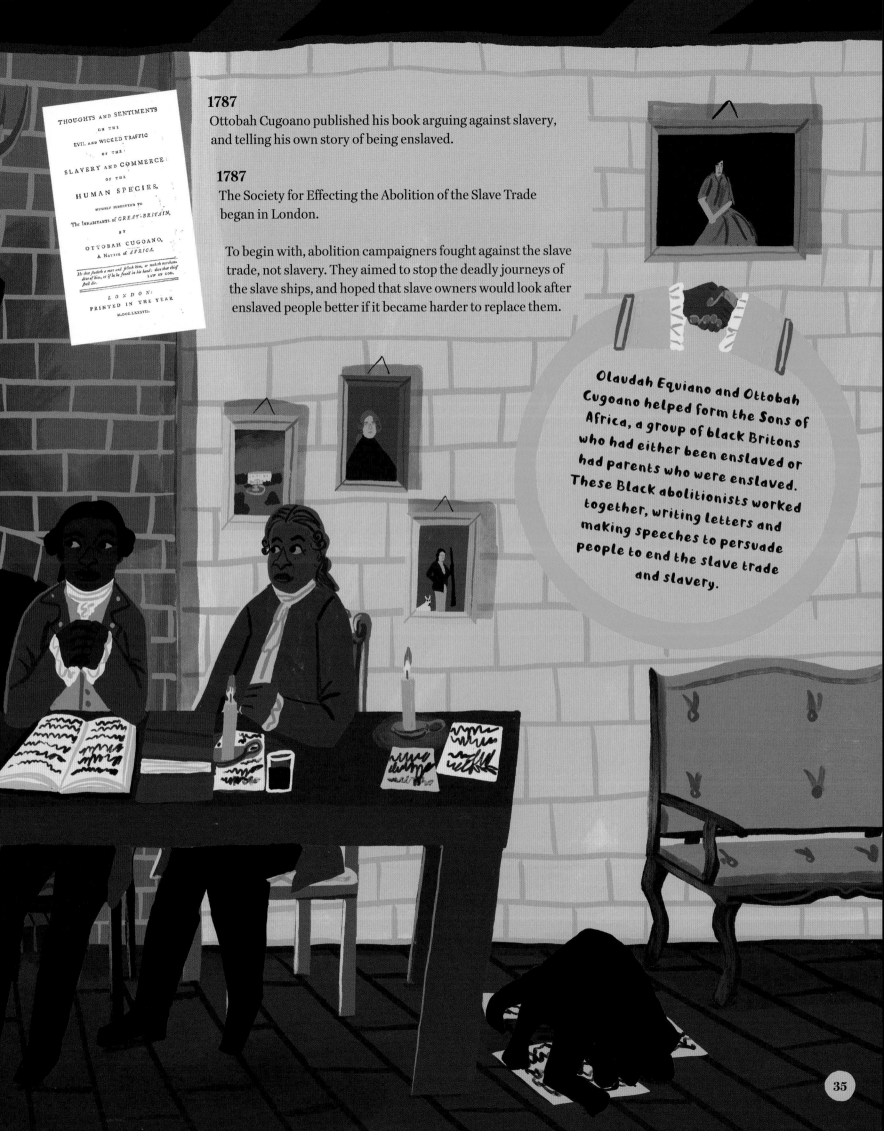

THOUGHTS AND SENTIMENTS
ON THE
EVIL AND WICKED TRAFFIC
OF THE
SLAVERY AND COMMERCE
OF THE
HUMAN SPECIES,
HUMBLY SUBMITTED TO
The Inhabitants of GREAT-BRITAIN,
BY
OTTOBAH CUGOANO,
A Native of AFRICA.

LONDON:
PRINTED IN THE YEAR
M.DCC.LXXXVII.

1787

Ottobah Cugoano published his book arguing against slavery, and telling his own story of being enslaved.

1787

The Society for Effecting the Abolition of the Slave Trade began in London.

To begin with, abolition campaigners fought against the slave trade, not slavery. They aimed to stop the deadly journeys of the slave ships, and hoped that slave owners would look after enslaved people better if it became harder to replace them.

Olaudah Equiano and Ottobah Cugoano helped form the Sons of Africa, a group of black Britons who had either been enslaved or had parents who were enslaved. These Black abolitionists worked together, writing letters and making speeches to persuade people to end the slave trade and slavery.

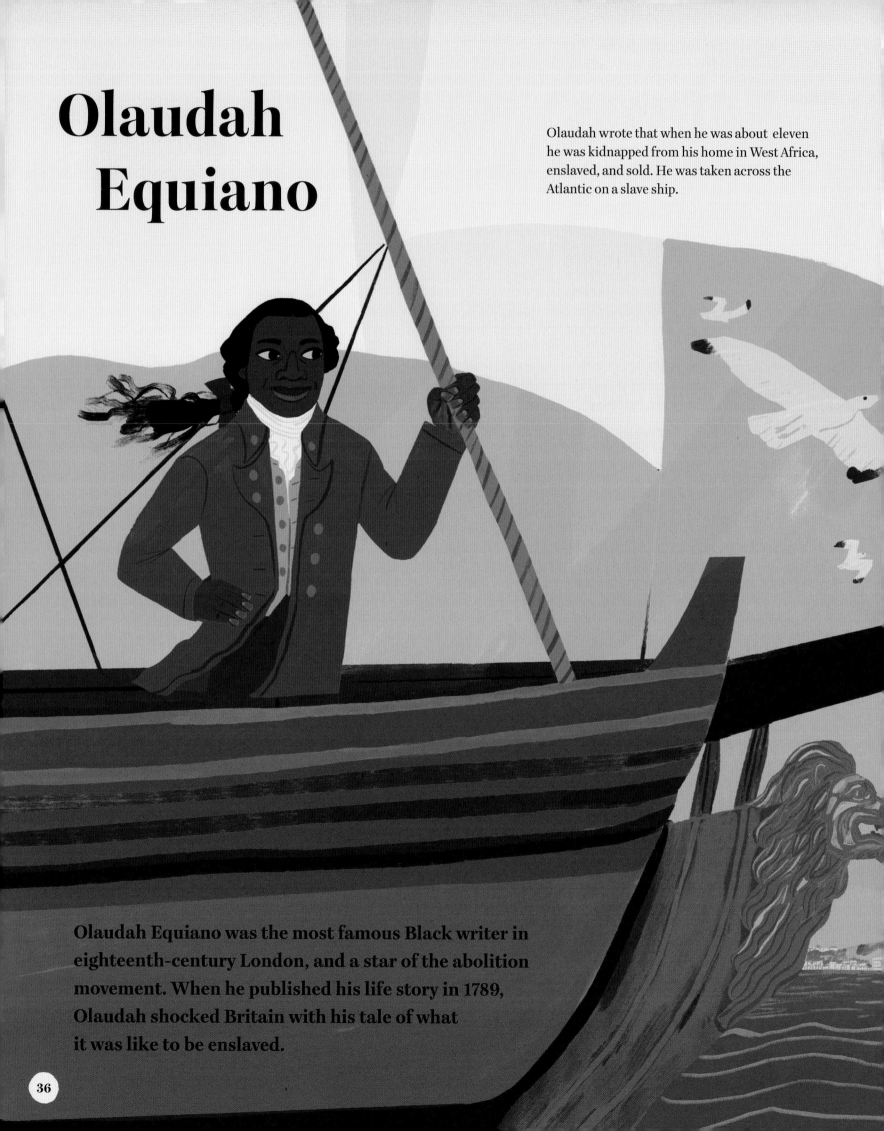

Olaudah Equiano

Olaudah wrote that when he was about eleven he was kidnapped from his home in West Africa, enslaved, and sold. He was taken across the Atlantic on a slave ship.

Olaudah Equiano was the most famous Black writer in eighteenth-century London, and a star of the abolition movement. When he published his life story in 1789, Olaudah shocked Britain with his tale of what it was like to be enslaved.

The book of Olaudah's life story made his readers feel the cruelty of slave ships and slavery. His powerful writing and national book tours made it a bestseller. The book made him famous, and also helped persuade British people that slavery was morally wrong.

Olaudah was bought by a Royal Navy officer, and went to sea with him. In the Navy, Olaudah learned to read and write and became a skilled sailor. He also became a Christian, and was baptized in London.

While he was enslaved by a different owner in the West Indies, Olaudah learned to be a businessman, buying and selling as he travelled. He made enough money to buy his freedom.

To earn a living, Olaudah went back to sea. He travelled the world, and even went on an expedition to the Arctic.

In the 1770s, Olaudah settled in London where he campaigned against slavery. He worked with other abolitionists like Granville Sharp and the Sons of Africa, and his name and face became famous.

Resistance and Rebellion

Abolitionists were not the only people working against slavery. Enslaved people resisted their enslavers in Africa, at sea, in Britain, and in the colonies. Many resisted by working slowly or by running away; others managed to join together to fight back.

Tacky's Revolt

A group of enslaved people in Jamaica fought against their enslavers in 1760. 'Tacky's Revolt' was the century's biggest slave rising in the British West Indies. It was named after the man who led enslaved people to take guns and ammunition from a fort. The British quickly stopped Tacky's revolt, but other rebels kept fighting for over a year.

Sam Sharpe's Rebellion

The rebellion led by Sam Sharpe in Jamaica in 1831 started out as a peaceful strike. A group of enslaved people refused to work unless they were paid wages. When the slave owners reacted violently, tens of thousands of enslaved people began to fight for their freedom. The British defeated the rebels, killing hundreds in Jamaica.

Haitian Revolution

The largest and only successful slave rebellion in history was in the French colony of Saint-Domingue (now Haiti). The French Revolution shook Europe in 1789, based on ideas of freedom and equality. Those ideas spread to France's colonies. Two years later, the enslaved people in Saint-Domingue rose up to take their own freedom.

General Toussaint L'Ouverture led the rebels to victory over the French and the British, and began the free Black republic of Haiti. Slavery was banned. Slave owners everywhere were shocked and scared that it was possible for enslaved people to fight and take back their freedom.

All through the time of Atlantic slavery, enslavers worried that the people they had enslaved would rise up against them.

Most rebellions were defeated, and the authorities took violent revenge. Still, each uprising inspired more enslaved people to rebel.

Each rebellion also scared the slave owners, and showed that the slavery system could not last forever.

Toussaint L'Ouverture

Abolitionists used all kinds of methods to get their message across. They published pamphlets and books, and held big public meetings where they showed the audience the chains used by the slave traders. Black people who had been enslaved, like Ottobah Cugoano, Olaudah Equiano and Mary Prince, published books telling their life stories and showing readers the awful truth of slavery.

Abolitionists collected signatures on petitions to show Parliament how many people wanted to end the slave trade.

Between 1787 and 1792, 1.5 million people signed petitions against the slave trade, at a time when there were only 12 million people living in Britain.

★ **1788**
Parliament made a law to limit the number of people a slave ship could carry, and to make sure a doctor on each ship kept records.

★ **1789**
Abolitionist MP William Wilberforce made his first speech against the slave trade in Parliament. He kept trying to get Parliament to vote against the slave trade for the next 18 years.

Elizabeth Heyrick was a teacher from Leicester, whose Quaker beliefs told her slavery was wrong. By the 1820s Elizabeth was not prepared to wait for slavery to end. She wrote a pamphlet called 'Immediate, not Gradual Abolition', and helped push the white abolition movement to faster action.

Women could not vote in elections in the eighteenth century, but they played a major role in the abolition campaign. They organized committees, campaigned, and promoted the sugar boycott: urging people not to buy or eat sugar that had been produced by enslaved people.

1791

The revolution of enslaved people in Saint-Domingue (modern Haiti) began. In the free Black republic of Haiti, slavery would be illegal.

1807

Parliament voted to end the slave trade by law.

1823

A new campaign began, aiming to end slavery itself.

1831

Sam Sharpe's rebellion in Jamaica made it clear that if slavery was not abolished, there would be another, even bigger, uprising.

1833

Parliament voted to end slavery.

1838

1 August: the enslaved people in the British Empire were finally freed.

When the British government abolished slavery, the slave owners demanded compensation money for the loss of their human property. The government agreed to pay the huge sum of twenty million pounds to the 46,000 slave owners. The former slaves received nothing.

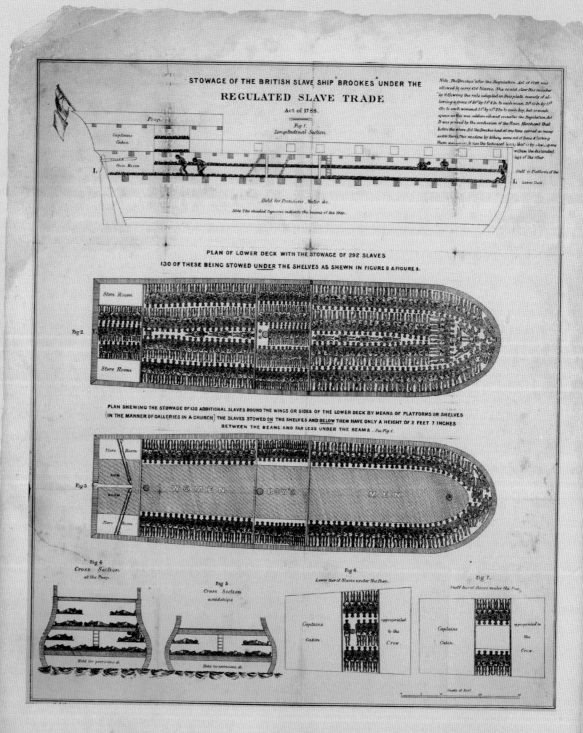

STOWAGE OF THE BRITISH SLAVE SHIP "BROOKES" UNDER THE
REGULATED SLAVE TRADE
Act of 1788.

PLAN OF LOWER DECK WITH THE STOWAGE OF 292 SLAVES
130 OF THESE BEING STOWED UNDER THE SHELVES AS SHEWN IN FIGURE B & FIGURE 5.

PLAN SHEWING THE STOWAGE OF 130 ADDITIONAL SLAVES ROUND THE WINGS OR SIDES OF THE LOWER DECK BY MEANS OF PLATFORMS OR SHELVES (IN THE MANNER OF GALLERIES IN A CHURCH) THE SLAVES STOWED ON THE SHELVES AND BELOW THEM HAVE ONLY A HEIGHT OF 2 FEET 7 INCHES BETWEEN THE BEAMS: AND FAR LESS UNDER THE BEAMS. See Fig 1.

Thomas Clarkson was a leader of the abolitionists, who campaigned all around the country. Thomas used a model of a slave ship called the Brooks to show how people were packed onto them in chains, and gave a copy of the model to William Wilberforce to use in Parliament. The abolitionists also produced a poster of the ship, which became one of the most famous images in the battle against the slave trade.

THE VICTORIANS

THE WEST AFRICA SQUADRON

It took more than laws to stop the slave trade. In 1808, once the trade was banned, the Royal Navy switched from protecting British slave ships to hunting them down. Britain had been the world's biggest slave-trading country in the North Atlantic. Now, it had an anti-slave-trade police force: the Royal Navy's West Africa Squadron.

The West Africa Squadron helped to stop British merchants from trading in slaves, although some British merchants still invested their money in businesses that relied on raw materials produced by enslaved people. Enormous numbers of slave ships from various countries still managed to cross the Atlantic in spite of the Squadron.

The West Africa Squadron operated for nearly sixty years. In that time, it managed to free about one hundred and sixty thousand people.

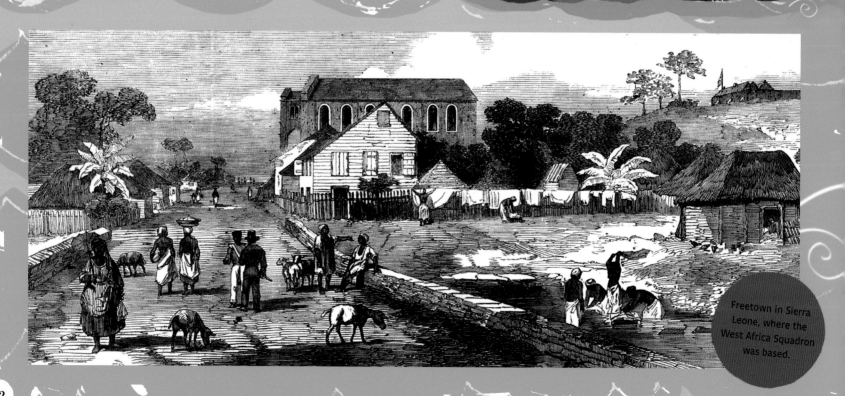

Freetown in Sierra Leone, where the West Africa Squadron was based.

Their most famous ship was called the *Black Joke*. Like many
of the Squadron's best ships, it was captured from slave traders,
who could afford faster ships than the Navy's.

In 1829, the *Black Joke* chased a bigger and better-armed Spanish slave
ship for thirty-one hours, day and night, and then freed the 466 people
held on board. The daring chase made headlines back home in Britain.
Some of the *Black Joke's* crew were Africans from the Kru people, who
used to make their living as fishermen and sailors. The West Africa
Squadron employed many skilled Kru seamen.

The people freed by the West Africa Squadron often made their home
in the city of Freetown, Sierra Leone. Freetown was home to Africans
from different places, with many languages and cultures. The city was
shaped by Britain and by the many thousands of people whose lives had
been turned upside down by the slave trade and the fight against it.

Sarah Forbes Bonetta

Sarah Forbes Bonetta was both African and British. She became a friend of Queen Victoria and a Black Victorian celebrity.

In 1849, Captain Frederick Forbes of the West Africa Squadron visited the Kingdom of Dahomey. His trip was part of the government's plan to replace the slave trade with legal trade between Britain and Africa, in goods like palm oil, cotton, or ivory. Forbes was sent to meet King Ghezo and persuade him to give up the slave trade. Dahomey had become rich through slavery, and not surprisingly Ghezo said no. Instead, he gave Frederick Forbes presents to take back to Queen Victoria, including a young enslaved girl of about seven years old.

On the way to England, the girl was given a new name: Sarah Forbes (after Captain Frederick) Bonetta (the name of the ship).

Sarah Forbes Bonetta met Queen Victoria, who liked her instantly and wrote in her diary that Sarah was 'sharp & intelligent'. The Queen paid for her to be educated in Freetown.

Back in England, Sarah was introduced to and married a successful Black businessman from Sierra Leone named James Pinson Labulo Davies. Their wedding in Brighton was reported in the newspapers, and a celebrity photographer took their picture (see the opposite page).

Sarah and James's daughter was named Victoria, and the Queen was her godmother. When Sarah died, the Queen paid for her daughter to go to school in England.

BLACK AMERICANS IN BRITAIN

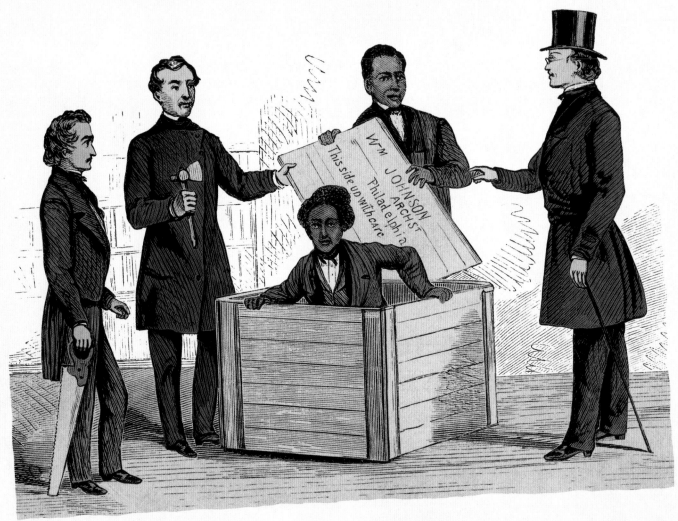

Many of the Black American speakers who toured Britain to get support for the campaign to end slavery had been enslaved themselves. They told their stories in towns and cities all around the country.

Henry 'Box' Brown was a star speaker who got his nickname from the dramatic way he freed himself: he had himself mailed in a wooden box to a city where slavery was illegal. Brown spent twenty-seven hours folded inside the box, which was less than a metre long.

When Henry 'Box' Brown toured Britain, he took his box with him and appeared from inside it on stage.

In 1840, campaigners met in London for the World Anti-Slavery Convention. They agreed that Britain had done a wonderful thing by abolishing slavery — and the next task was to end slavery all around the world. There were still more than two million enslaved people in the USA, a country with close links to Britain. British and American campaigners began to work together to end slavery.

FREDERICK DOUGLASS

was the most famous Black American speaker to tour Victorian Britain. After escaping from slavery, Douglass became a lecturer and campaigner. He came to Britain to speak and raise money. He also came to get further away from the man who still legally owned him, until friends in Britain helped to buy his freedom.

SARAH PARKER REMOND

was a free-born, educated woman who came to Britain in 1859 and gave lectures on the evils of slavery, including how enslaved women suffered. Sarah also campaigned for women's right to vote, and later became a doctor.

Musicians from America also brought a craze for Black American music to British fans.

THE BOHEE BROTHERS

were American banjo stars, who were said to have taught the Prince of Wales to play.

THE FISK JUBILEE SINGERS

sang to packed audiences all over Britain in the 1870s and 1880s, making 'spiritual' songs famous. Their hits included 'Nobody Knows The Trouble I See' and 'Swing Low Sweet Chariot'.

The Industrial Revolution

When I was at school, I learned how the Industrial Revolution made Victorian Britain rich. I learned about the huge factories, the rich men who owned them, the machines that were invented, and the children who worked in the factories and mills.

Two of the most important products of the Industrial Revolution were cotton thread and cotton cloth. But what nobody ever mentioned when I was learning about the mills was where the cotton came from.

Most of the cotton worked in British mills came from the southern states of the USA, where the climate was right for the cotton plant.

It was grown and picked by enslaved people.

The cotton was brought by ship to Liverpool and then taken to mills in Lancashire, in northern England, to be turned into yarn and cloth. Thousands of mills in Lancashire processed cotton, and the city of Manchester became known as 'Cottonopolis'. By the 1860s, cotton was a main export of the United Kingdom.

I was not taught that these industries were partly powered by slavery from the beginning. Many of the factories were built using money made by investing in the slave trade. Trading in enslaved people and the goods they produced had made British businessmen enormously rich, and helped them develop new ways of doing business, new banks to handle their money, and new skills to run production on a massive scale. All this gave extra power and speed to the Industrial Revolution.

Even though the Victorians were proud that Britain had abolished slavery, British businesses still relied on cotton grown by enslaved people. Lancashire and the southern USA were part of the same system. This meant that when a war began in America, it also shook the north of England.

49

The American Civil War

The American colonies which had gained independence from Britain became the first of the states to join together in a union known as the United States of America. In 1861, some states left the union and a war began between the two sides. Most of the states still in the Union were northern states where slavery was illegal, while the southern Confederate states used enslaved people to work the plantations which brought them their wealth.

● Union (northern states)
● Confederate (southern states)
● Territories

The northern states blocked ships from using southern ports in the war. This meant that cotton could no longer be sent from America to Britain. By the end of 1862 the British factories were running out of cotton and hundreds of thousands of people in northern England were out of work. This was called the 'Cotton Famine'.

The British government decided not to take sides in the American Civil War, but many British people did.

Merchants in the port of Liverpool, where slave-produced cotton was unloaded, mostly supported the South. They found ways around the blockade, built ships for the South, and sent them guns.

Some British mill workers and mill owners backed the North because they believed that slavery was wrong. They did this even though they were suffering without the cotton which was being held up by northern forces. Support for the North was especially strong in Rochdale, Lancashire, where workers had a tradition of campaigning against slavery. In thanks, the North sent a ship full of food for the people of Lancashire.

PROCLAMATION OF EMANCIPATION

President Abraham Lincoln announced that the slaves would be freed if the North won the Civil War.

A group of workers from Manchester wrote to the President to say that they supported him, and that the war and their own poverty would be worth it if it meant Black Americans would be free.

The North did indeed win the war, and banned slavery across the USA in January 1865.

The Scramble for Africa

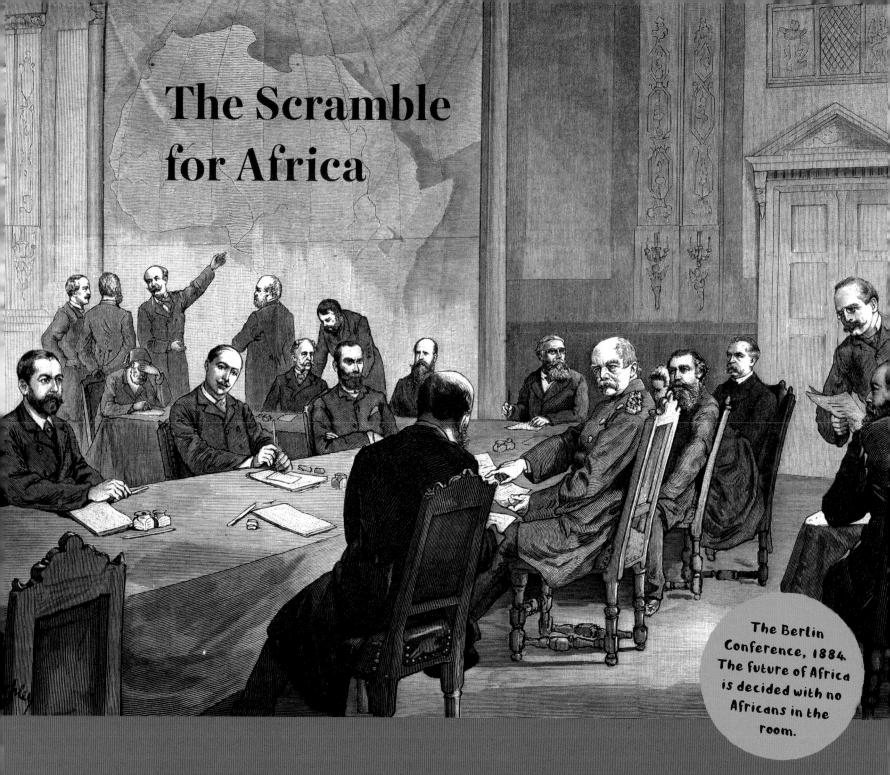

The Berlin Conference, 1884. The future of Africa is decided with no Africans in the room.

In the 'Scramble for Africa', European countries raced to grab land and power. Having African colonies would help each colonizing country to get rich and compete with its European neighbours. Britain also said that if it had more power in Africa, it could end slavery there.

The leaders of Europe, the USA and the Ottoman Empire met in 1884 to make a plan for colonizing Africa. No African leaders were invited.

Back in Britain, the stories of explorers, hunters and soldiers in Africa were told as heroic adventures. Maps showed the British Empire all around the world, coloured in pink. It was exciting for people to feel that their country could rule so much of the world, and it seemed to prove that the British were special.

European scientists studied people from different parts of Africa as if they were new discoveries. Some Africans came to Britain as a kind of museum exhibit. Massive colonial exhibitions were held, often with African villages where visitors could watch Africans acting out everyday life. The 'villages' were less real than they seemed. Some of the Africans were professional performers who spoke English, wore European clothes, and travelled around different exhibitions as their job.

Africa, 1914

Legend:
- BRITISH
- FRENCH
- SPANISH
- PORTUGUESE
- BELGIAN
- GERMAN
- ITALIAN
- INDEPENDENT

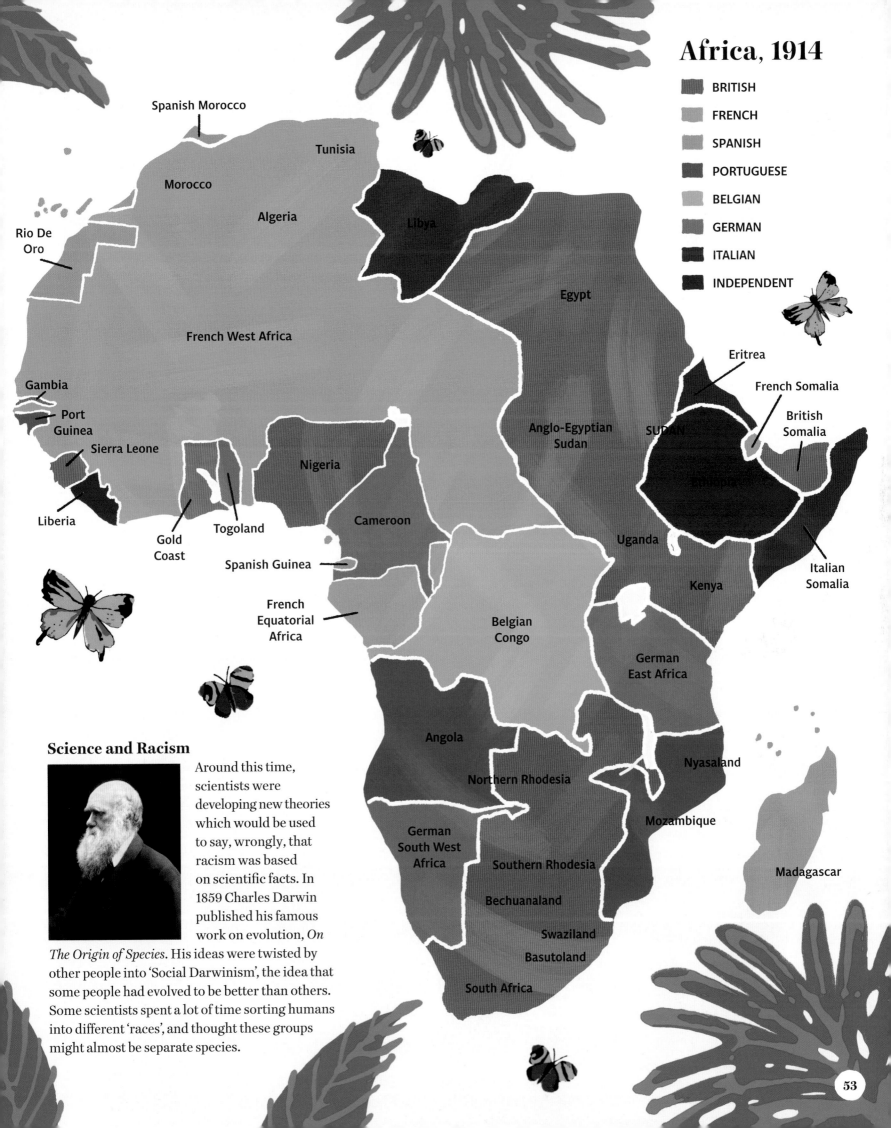

Spanish Morocco

Tunisia

Morocco

Algeria

Libya

Rio De Oro

Egypt

French West Africa

Eritrea

French Somalia

Gambia

Anglo-Egyptian Sudan

SUDAN

British Somalia

Port Guinea

Sierra Leone

Nigeria

Ethiopia

Liberia

Cameroon

Uganda

Italian Somalia

Gold Coast

Togoland

Spanish Guinea

Kenya

French Equatorial Africa

Belgian Congo

German East Africa

Angola

Nyasaland

Northern Rhodesia

Mozambique

German South West Africa

Southern Rhodesia

Madagascar

Bechuanaland

Swaziland

Basutoland

South Africa

Science and Racism

Around this time, scientists were developing new theories which would be used to say, wrongly, that racism was based on scientific facts. In 1859 Charles Darwin published his famous work on evolution, *On The Origin of Species*. His ideas were twisted by other people into 'Social Darwinism', the idea that some people had evolved to be better than others. Some scientists spent a lot of time sorting humans into different 'races', and thought these groups might almost be separate species.

Map of the British Empire 1886

This map was produced in 1886, when the British Empire was huge and growing. It celebrates the global reach of the Empire. The countries which were part of the British Empire are coloured in pink.

The illustrations around the map show people from all over the world brought together as part of the British Empire. Maps and pictures like this could make the Empire look exciting and full of opportunities.

There are some clues in the pictures that the artist may not have thought the Empire was perfect – like the worker bending under a heavy load in the bottom left of the frame.

FROM LEFT TO RIGHT: Sebele I of the Kwêna people, Bathoen I of the Bangwaketse, Khama III of the BagammaNgwato and the Reverend Charles Willoughby of the London Missionary Society.

In 1895 a group of three kings from Bechuanaland, now known as Botswana, made an extraordinary royal visit to Britain. It was part of King Khama III's plan to stand up to the colonialist who wanted to take their lands.

The man King Khama was worried about was Cecil Rhodes, Prime Minister of the Cape Colony in today's South Africa. Rhodes believed the British were superior to other people and that the world would be better if Britain ruled more of it. He dreamed of British land in Africa all the way from its southern tip to Egypt in the north. Bechuanaland was part of Rhodes' plan. It was already a 'protectorate' of the British government, but Rhodes wanted his own private company to take over Bechuanaland and sell land to white settlers.

For weeks, the kings travelled around Britain, attending events, giving speeches and becoming celebrities. Finally, they made a deal with the government to keep Rhodes out of Bechuanaland. Khama had achieved his aim.

BLACK VICTORIANS

Here are some of the Black Victorians who built their lives in Britain and the Empire.

Fanny Eaton's face became famous in Victorian Britain, even if her name was not. Fanny was born in Jamaica; her father was white, and her mother had been enslaved. Fanny came to London with her mother. She worked as a cleaner, a housekeeper, and a cook – and also as an artists' model. Her beauty and her dark skin made her stand out. Because famous artists chose to paint her, you can still see her face in art galleries.

Jimmy Durham was given his name by soldiers from the Durham Light Infantry regiment, who adopted him as a child while they were fighting in Sudan in 1885. Jimmy went to England and India with the British army, and settled in the north-east of England.

Alice Kinloch was born in today's South Africa in 1863, and came to Britain in the 1890s. Alice fought for the rights of Black people in South Africa who were suffering under colonial rule. She helped set up the African Association to give Black people in Britain and elsewhere a stronger voice.

Mary Seacole is today one of the most famous Black Victorians. Born in Jamaica, Mary called herself 'Creole', meaning mixed race. Mary grew up in her mother's boarding house for army officers, and learned her mother's traditional herbal medicine. She is most famous for the British Hotel she ran for officers and soldiers in the Crimean War, providing food, drink and care for the wounded.

Pablo Fanque was the stage name of William Darby, a circus star from Norwich whose father was African. Pablo was an expert horse rider and trapeze artist, and ran his own circus. His name became famous again when the Beatles released a song called 'Being For The Benefit of Mr Kite', inspired by a poster for one of Pablo Fanque's shows.

THE FIRST WORLD WAR

The First World War began in the summer of 1914 and quickly became a clash between empires. Soldiers from all over the world fought and died, including men from the British colonies in Africa and the West Indies. The first and last fighting of the war happened in Africa, between soldiers fighting for British land forces and Germany in their colonies there.

The British army in Africa needed to travel many miles with their weapons and kit, so they recruited hundreds of thousands African carriers.

Regiments of African soldiers in the British Army also fought against the Germans in East Africa.

The British West Indies Regiment fought in Egypt and the Middle East. When West Indian soldiers from the regiment were sent to France they found that instead of fighting, they were mostly put to work, doing jobs like digging trenches and moving supplies. It was important and dangerous work, but it was not the fighting they had trained for.

Soldiers of the British West Indies Regiment in France, 1916

West Indian soldiers stacking shells, 1917

Walter Tull before the war, in Tottenham Hotspur kit

A few Black soldiers managed to join British army regiments alongside white men and fought with them in Europe, if the officers in charge chose to let them.

The most famous Black British soldier of the First World War was Walter Tull. Born in Kent, his father was from Barbados. 26-year-old Tull was already a famous footballer when he joined the army in 1914. He was quickly promoted, and went to France to fight.

He became an officer, even though army rules said that all officers should be 'of pure European descent' – meaning white. The rules could be bent for the right person. Walter Tull led his men as a second lieutenant until March 1918, when he was killed in action in France.

Dr John Alcindor

Dr John Alcindor from Trinidad applied to join the Royal Army Medical Corps when the war began.

Even though he had trained in Edinburgh and worked as one of the first Black doctors in London for years, he was turned down.

Instead, Dr Alcindor signed up as a volunteer with the Red Cross. He worked at railway stations in London, treating wounded soldiers as they arrived from the front line, and the Red Cross awarded him a medal in thanks.

Fighting stopped in November 1918. The war had changed the world, and thrown people from all over the British Empire together in new ways. But Black soldiers, sailors and workers had also been reminded that they were seen as less important than white people.

In July 1919, a victory parade was held in London to celebrate the official end of the war. Nearly fifteen thousand service people from the British Empire marched through the city. But the African and West Indian regiments which had fought for Britain were not invited to take part.

After the war, times were hard. British soldiers came home to find that there were not enough jobs or houses for them. It was easy to blame this on immigrants, and especially on the Black people who were often paid less and whose skin colour made them stand out. Thousands of Black people had come to Britain in the war; some were sailors who had brought food and weapons which Britain needed in wartime. Others had come to work in the factories.

In 1919, fights began to break out between white people and Black sailors and their families in port cities like Glasgow and Liverpool. The fighting turned into riots, with violent crowds attacking Black people and raiding their homes.

The authorities often saw the Black people living in these cities as the cause of the trouble and new more restrictive laws were passed.

The Liverpool Tribune
1919

MURDER!

CHARLES WOOTTON WAS A SAILOR FROM BERMUDA WHO WAS KILLED IN A RIOT IN LIVERPOOL IN 1919.

THE SECOND WORLD WAR

Thousands of Africans and West Indians served in the British forces during the Second World War. The war also brought many more Black people to Britain than ever before.

Before the war, the British Army, Royal Navy and Royal Air Force all had different rules that made it difficult or impossible for Black men to serve. Campaigners argued against this, and after the war began in 1939, the government agreed to relax the rules.

Around 372,000 Africans served in the British forces during the war. The African regiments of the British Army mostly fought in Africa and Asia.

More than 16,000 West Indians served in the British forces, including in the Royal Air Force, the Royal Canadian Air Force, the Women's Auxiliary Air Force and the Auxiliary Territorial Service (the women's branch of the British Army). Men from the West Indies and from Africa also served in the merchant navy, bringing food and other vital supplies to Britain.

Other West Indians came to Britain to do war work, like the lumberjacks from British Honduras who worked in Scottish forests, or the electricians and engineers who came to Liverpool from the West Indies.

NATIONAL REGISTRATION IDENTITY CARD

Name: Ulric Cross

Country of origin: Trinidad

History: Came to Britain in 1941 to join the RAF.

He wanted adventure and to fight the Nazis.

Ulric flew eighty bombing missions to Europe and earned two military awards, the Distinguished Flying Cross and the Distinguished Service Order.

Name: Lilian Bader (born Lilian Bailey)

Country of origin: Liverpool, UK

History: Lilian became one of the first Black women to join the British armed forces. When the war began, she got a job in a forces canteen, but was asked to leave because her father had been born in Barbados. Later, Lilian heard of West Indians joining the RAF, and so she joined the Women's Auxiliary Air Force and became an instrument repairer. Lilian married a Black soldier named Ramsay Bader, and left the WAAF in 1944 to have their first child.

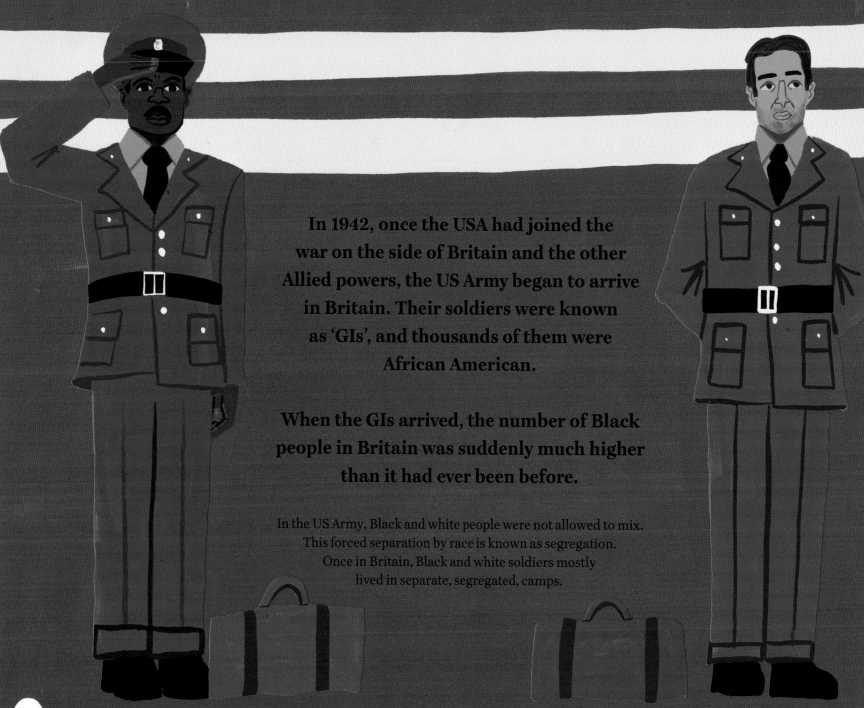

In 1942, once the USA had joined the war on the side of Britain and the other Allied powers, the US Army began to arrive in Britain. Their soldiers were known as 'GIs', and thousands of them were African American.

When the GIs arrived, the number of Black people in Britain was suddenly much higher than it had ever been before.

In the US Army, Black and white people were not allowed to mix. This forced separation by race is known as segregation. Once in Britain, Black and white soldiers mostly lived in separate, segregated, camps.

Segregation was not part of British law, and British people did not always agree with it. Many white American soldiers felt it was up to them to enforce the rules. One white British woman who served Black GIs in her bar had a complaint from a white GI. She replied that she would carry on serving her Black customers, because 'their money is as good as yours, and we prefer their company'.

Some white US soldiers attacked Black GIs who met or dated white British women. Some British people also disapproved of these relationships. The children of white British women and Black GIs faced discrimination after the war, and many of them were sent to children's homes.

On June 6, 1944, known as D-Day, most of the US Army left Britain as part of the invasion of Nazi-occupied western Europe.

By 1945 there were probably fewer than 20,000 Black people in Britain, but politicians did not want more coming to the country. West Indians were not aware of this; during the war they had been largely welcomed in Britain to serve in the armed forces and work in the factories. When they went home to the West Indies after 1945, many found it impossible to get jobs. Some decided to return to Britain.

WINDRUSH TO TODAY

Although there had been Black people living in Britain for centuries, after the end of the Second World War far more Black people started to come to Britain and make their homes there.

Britain needed workers to rebuild the country after the war. Many people in the West Indies needed jobs. They had the legal right to live and work in the UK as citizens of the British Empire, and some had even fought for Britain in the war.

1945
The Second World War ends.

1948
A law called the British Nationality Act gives people from the British Empire the right to come to Britain to live. The government expects most of them to be white people from Canada, South Africa, Australia and New Zealand, not people from Jamaica, India or Nigeria.

1948
June: the *Empire Windrush* ship arrives from Jamaica.

1948
The National Health Service is created. The NHS will recruit thousands of nurses from the West Indies in its early years.

1956
London Transport begins to hire workers directly from the West Indies.

1958
Violence breaks out in Nottingham and in the area of Notting Hill in London when white gangs attack Black people and their homes.

EMPIRE

LON

The *Empire Windrush* was a ship which became famous for bringing hundreds of passengers from the West Indies to Britain in 1948.

The 'Caribbean Carnival' held in north London in 1959 was the beginning of the famous Notting Hill Carnival.

1959

Claudia Jones organizes the first version of the Notting Hill Carnival, to celebrate the Caribbean community.

1962

Parliament says that people coming to the UK from the former British Empire to work will need employment vouchers. Race is not mentioned, but the government gives out fewer vouchers for jobs which are mostly done by Black people.

1963

The Bristol Bus Boycott calls attention to the local bus company's refusal to hire Black or Asian workers. The boycott forces the company to change the rules.

1965

The government introduces the first Race Relations Act, beginning to make racial discrimination illegal. In 1968 another act bans discrimination in housing, jobs, and banking.

1968

Conservative politician Enoch Powell makes a famous speech warning of disaster if Black and Asian people keep coming to Britain. Public support for Powell, and rising racist attacks, make Black and Asian people feel much less safe.

The ship gave its name to the 'Windrush Generation': the people who travelled from the West Indies to make a home in Britain from 1948 to the early 1970s.

These Windrush passengers were housed in an air raid shelter under a tube station in Clapham, south London, while they looked for work.

Since the arrival of the *Windrush*, Black British people have played a huge part in shaping British culture. Here are just a few of those leaders, thinkers, artists, famous faces and experts who have helped to build modern Britain.

②

③

①

⑥

⑤

⑦

⑧

4

9

10

1. **Benjamin Zephaniah:** Benjamin is a poet, who grew up in Birmingham and started writing poems as a teenager. His politics are at the heart of his poetry. Benjamin is a vegan and a campaigner for animal rights.

2. **Dr Harold Moody:** Harold came to London from Jamaica in 1904 to study medicine, but as a Black doctor he was denied work in hospitals. He became a GP and formed the League of Coloured Peoples, to fight for the rights of Black people in Britain.

3. **Sir Lenny Henry:** Lenny is a comedian, actor, writer and campaigner who helped to start the charity event Comic Relief in 1985. He became famous as a stand-up comic, and has recently been recognized for his stage acting in Shakespeare plays. Lenny campaigns for more diversity in the British media.

4. **Claudia Jones:** Claudia was a journalist who campaigned against racism. She began the *West Indian Gazette* in 1958, the year of the Notting Hill riots. She then began the Notting Hill Carnival as a way to celebrate and support the West Indian community.

5. **Baroness Doreen Lawrence:** In 1993, Doreen's son Stephen Lawrence was murdered in a racist attack. Doreen would not let her son be forgotten. Together with Stephen's father Neville, Doreen has campaigned ever since for justice for Stephen, for change in the police force, and for opportunities for all.

6. **Sam King:** After serving in the RAF in the Second World War, Sam came to Britain on the *Windrush*. He became a politician and campaigner, and was the first Black mayor of the London borough of Southwark.

7. **Dame Shirley Bassey:** Shirley is a proudly Welsh singer who was one of the first Black British musicians to become an international star. She sang several theme songs for James Bond films, including *Goldfinger* and *Diamonds Are Forever*.

8. **Tessa Sanderson :** Tessa is an athlete who competed for Britain in the javelin and heptathlon. In 1984, she was the first Black British woman to win an Olympic gold medal, and became the first British person to win an Olympic throwing event. In all, she competed at six Olympic Games.

9. **Sir Lewis Hamilton:** Lewis has been the first and only Black driver in Formula One racing, winning World Championships and Grands Prix. He has changed the sport with his style, politics, and attitude, and is one of the world's highest-paid sports stars.

10. **Altheia Jones-LeCointe:** Altheia was a leader of the British Black Panthers group which fought against racial discrimination in the late 1960s and early 1970s.

4

8

10

1. **Baroness Patricia Scotland:** Patricia is a lawyer with a long line of 'firsts'. She was the first Black woman, and youngest ever woman, to be made a Queen's Counsel (a type of senior lawyer). She has had a seat in the House of Lords since 1997. In 2007 she became the UK's first ever female Attorney General, the government's legal advisor.

2. **Stormzy:** Stormzy is one of twenty-first century Britain's biggest-selling musicians. He was the first grime artist to have a number one in the UK album charts. Stormzy often talks about politics and racism and he supports charities fighting for justice, and publishes books.

3. **Andrea Levy:** Andrea was an author whose father came to Britain on the *Empire Windrush*. Her novel *Small Island* was a prize-winning bestseller about the experiences of the Windrush generation.

4. **Stuart Hall:** Stuart was a writer, teacher, professor and thinker. He wrote about race in Britain and took 'popular culture' like film and TV seriously, and thought its messages were worth studying.

5. **Malorie Blackman:** Malorie is a bestselling author who writes for children and young people. Some of her best known books are the Noughts & Crosses series, which have been adapted for theatre and TV. She was the first Black writer to be named UK Children's Laureate.

6. **Paul Gilroy:** Paul is a historian and writer who works on Black British culture. His ideas about race have changed the way we talk about it.

7. **Baroness Floella Benjamin:** Floella came to England from Trinidad as a child in 1960, and became famous as a children's TV presenter. She also acts and writes books, and sits in Parliament, in the House of Lords.

8. **Olive Morris:** Olive was a teenager in Brixton when she was arrested for getting involved when she saw the police beating a Black man. She soon began organizing Black women's groups, leading protests, studying, travelling, and fighting for a fairer world.

9. **Marcus Rashford:** Marcus achieved footballing success at an early age, as a star player for Manchester United and for England. He is also famous for campaigning for change on homelessness and child poverty.

10. **Dame Elizabeth Anionwu:** Elizabeth is a professor of nursing, who chose her career after a nurse was one of the few people to treat her kindly at the children's home where she grew up. Elizabeth became the first nurse to specialize in sickle cell and thalassemia, conditions which mostly affect Black people.

Since the 1980s there have been many more Black people coming to Britain. Today, around three in every hundred people in the UK are Black.

BLACK LIVES MATTER

SAY THEIR NAMES

WE WANT JUSTICE

BLACK MAT

1981
April: London's Metropolitan Police begin an operation against street crime in Brixton, south London, home to a large Black community. They use the hated 'sus' law to stop and search anyone they suspect might be going to commit a crime. In response, young Black people riot in Brixton and in parts of other British cities.

1981
A house fire kills thirteen young Black people at a birthday party in New Cross, south London. Their families suggest it is a racist attack, but the police refuse to investigate properly. Thousands of people march in protest.

1993
Stephen Lawrence, a Black teenager, is killed by a gang of white men. An official inquiry finds later that the police did not investigate the murder properly because of institutional racism.

BLM

WE WAN

Black culture has transformed Britishness through sport, music, cinema, fashion art, books, television and more. But discrimination is still everywhere, including in education, jobs, policing, and health care. Recently a new generation has begun to look again at their shared history and to speak out against injustice.

2012
At the opening ceremony of the London Olympic Games, the arrival of the *Windrush* is celebrated alongside other great moments in British history.

2013
The government begins to pass laws to make Britain a 'hostile environment' for illegal immigrants, meaning it would be harder for them to stay in the country.

2018
The 'Windrush Scandal' is uncovered. Thousands of people from the West Indies who came to the UK mostly in the 1960s and 1970s have had their British citizenship taken away. Some have been sent 'back' to countries they have not visited since they were children.

2020
Black Lives Matter protests spread across the world following the murder of George Floyd by police in the USA. Thousands of people in Britain protest against racism. In Bristol, protestors pull down the statue of slave trader Edward Colston and dump it in the harbour.

AFTERWORD

I hope this book has helped you to see how Black British history is an important part of British history.

When I was a child, the stories contained within this book were not taught in my school. Most people, back then, never had a chance to learn about the Black people from the past who made their homes in Britain, or those who were enslaved by British slave traders or whose homelands were made part of the British Empire. Black British history is no longer invisible, instead it is celebrated and understood as an important part of British history.

It gives me hope to see young people learning more about Black British history today, whether in school or through new books, websites and television programmes. There is so much more to learn, and so many more stories still to uncover. I hope that you will carry on learning about this history, and that you find it as fascinating and inspiring as I have.

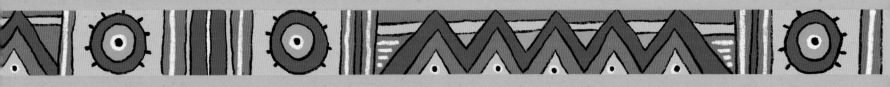

Glossary

- **Abolitionists** a group of people who campaigned to end slavery.

- **Act (of Parliament)** a piece of law, which starts as a bill, becomes an act once it has been agreed on by Parliament and had formal agreement from the Queen or King.

- **American Patriots** Americans who were rebelling against British rule during the late 1700s (around the time of the American Revolutionary War).

- **Atlantic Slave Trade** the period between 1640–1807 where around three and a half million people from Africa were enslaved and taken to America and the West Indies by the British.

- **Bill (government)** the formal proposal for a new law. If a bill is passed (agreed on) by Parliament it becomes an act.

- **Blockade** the act of blocking off a certain place so that food, people and other goods cannot enter, especially when a port is blocked by an enemy navy in war.

- **Boycott** to give up or avoid something for social or political reasons, including avoiding buying certain goods.

- **British Empire** the group of countries (colonies) that the British ruled.

- **Citizen** a person who is a legal member of a country, state, or empire, with rights of citizenship.

- **Colonialism** a system of getting and ruling over colonies by a more powerful country, and the ideas and attitudes that go with it.

- **Colonize** to make a new colony, or to get control over another country.

- **Colony** a group of people who settle in a new place but are still ruled by their homeland; the place they settle stays a colony as long as it is ruled by the colonizing country.

- **Discrimination** unfair treatment based on unreasonable ideas about a person or group.

- **Empire** a large group of places controlled by one powerful country or ruler or government.

- **Enslavement** making someone a slave; owning them and forcing them to work.

- **GI** a slang term for a US soldier.

- **Immigrant** a person who comes to live permanently in a foreign country.

- **Institutional racism** racial discrimination which comes from systems and ideas in an organization.

- **Interpreter** a person who translates between people speaking different languages.

- **Middle Passage** the horrific voyage that enslaved Africans were forced to take across the Atlantic Ocean.

- **Migrant** a person who moves from one country to another.

- **Moor** an old term meaning 'person from North Africa'; also used in the past to mean a Black person.

- **Nationality** the fact of being a citizen of a particular nation (country), recognized by the law.

- **Ottoman Empire** a state that controlled a large part of Northern Africa, Western Asia and South Eastern Europe between the fourteenth and early twentieth centuries.

- **Petition** a written request signed by many people and addressed to the government or other people in power.

- **Plantation** a large estate or piece of land used for farming crops on a large scale, such as cotton, tea or sugar cane.

- **Protectorate** a country or area that is protected or managed by another, usually more powerful, country.

- **Quakers** a religious group who believe God can be found in everyone and work for justice and equality.

- **Race Relations Acts** a set of British laws that made certain forms of racism illegal.

- **Racism** a system of unfair treatment based on the false belief that some racial or ethnic groups are better or worse than others.

- **Regiment** a large group of soldiers in an army.

- **Royal African Company** an English company that traded enslaved people.

- **Segregation** a system that forces people from different races to be separate from one another.

- **Settlement** a place which has recently been colonized by settlers from another country.

- **Social Darwinism** a theory used to justify political racism, based on Charles Darwin's theory of evolution but rejected by Darwin. 'Social Darwinism' says that some groups of people have evolved to be better than others.

- **Sons of Africa** a group of Black British abolitionists, who had either been enslaved themselves or who were the children of enslaved parents.

- **Sugar cane** a plant from which sugar is extracted.

- **Sus law** a British law that allowed the Police to stop and search anyone merely on the suspicion that they intended to commit a crime.

- **West Africa Squadron** a part of the British Royal Navy which chased slave ships after the slave trade was abolished from 1808.

- **West Indies** a term coined by colonizing European powers to refer to the islands of the Caribbean.

A NOTE ON WORDS

Science cannot be used to divide humans up neatly into races like 'Black', 'white' and 'mixed', though many people have tried. But those races do exist in people's heads and in the societies we live in, so it's important that we talk about them even if it's sometimes uncomfortable.

Because language is always changing, it can be hard to know which terms to use to talk about race. Here are my reasons for a couple of the choices I have made about words in this book.

I write **Black** with a capital B to make it clear that I'm writing about a group of people with shared African heritage and culture, not just a colour.

I use the term **'enslaved person'** more than 'slave', to remind us that people living under slavery were human. Slavery was a state forced on people, not a part of who they were.

ABOUT THE AUTHOR AND ILLUSTRATORS

David Olusoga – Author

David Olusoga is a British-Nigerian historian, broadcaster and BAFTA award-winning presenter and filmmaker. He is Professor of Public History at the University of Manchester and a regular contributor to the *Guardian, Observer, New Statesman* and *BBC History Magazine*. He was a contributor to *The Oxford Companion to Black British History*. In 2019 he was awarded an OBE for services to history and community integration.

Melleny Taylor – Illustrator

Melleny Taylor was a secondary school art & design teacher before becoming an illustrator. She enjoys working with a variety of materials – using a range of mixed media from pencil crayons to inks, from watercolours to sticks from the garden! In recent times she has moved into the digital world.

Jake Alexander – Illustrator

Jake Alexander is an illustrator from the South of England. In 2019 he won both the Macmillan Prize and the Creative Conscience Gold Medal with an early version of *We Want Our Books*. He often makes work based on popular culture and current events, having created a Star-Wars-themed zine and portraits of public figures such as Taika Waititi and Alexandria Ocasio-Cortez.

David Williams – Type Designer

David grew up in the city of Manchester, UK. After graduating he returned to Manchester and set up his business, Manchester Type, which creates new typefaces and develops existing fonts for an international client base. David created the typefaces **Mansa** and **Evert Sans** which we have used in this book. A typeface is a family of fonts each made up of letters, symbols and punctuation that share the same design characteristics.

Jo Foster – Editorial

Jo Foster has worked in TV production making history documentaries, and now writes about history for children. Her books include the History Spies series, *Why Would A Dog Need A Parachute?*, and museum guidebooks for the National Trust and Imperial War Museum. She lives in a house on top of a Roman burial ground and would love to know who's down there.